MANCHESTER

From Old Photographs

ERIC KRIEGER

AMBERLEY

First published 2019

Amberley Publishing
The Hill, Stroud
Gloucestershire, GL5 4EP

www.amberley-books.com

British Library Cataloguing in Publication Data.

A catalogue record for this book is available from the British Library.

ISBN 978 1 4456 9133 6 (print)
ISBN 978 1 4456 9134 3 (ebook)

Origination by Amberley Publishing.
Printed in the UK.

Contents

Introduction

Photography is considered to have begun as a practical and commercial activity in 1839. That year the process discovered by a Frenchman, Louis Daguerre, was announced to the world. Studios producing so-called daguerreotypes were subsequently licensed in London and the English provinces, including one at Manchester in 1841. A trade card advert from 1842 announced a 'Photographic & Daguerreotype Portrait Gallery, Ducie Place'. This street disappeared when the Royal Exchange was extended towards Cross Street later in the century. Other photographic processes and formats were introduced during the nineteenth century.

One such photographic format was the *carte de visite*. This was a small photograph stuck on a stiff card. The card was often used by the photographer to advertise the studio and business. These *cartes de visite* became popular and stimulated the growth in numbers of studios during the 1850s and 1860s. Not only were portraits taken, but *cartes* also documented landscapes and urban scenes. These were sold in much the same way that picture postcards later served as souvenirs of places visited. One such Manchester photographer who produced topographical *cartes de visite* in the 1860s was Helmut Petschler. He was German-born, living and working in Manchester, where there was a large German community. Petschler had a studio on Market Street, and not only did he photograph views in the city, but also at other northern locations.

In 1855, the Manchester Photographic Society was founded. The group included members of the Manchester Literary and Philosophical Society and shared the same address – then on George Street. A local trade directory from 1863 reveals that the photographic society's then president was the Bishop of Manchester. Photography was acknowledged at the historically important Art Treasures Exhibition, held at Old Trafford in 1857, where a section was given over to the youthful art form.

One member of the Manchester Photographic Society was James Mudd. He was born in 1821 at Halifax, and worked in Manchester as a textile pattern designer with his brother Robert. The brothers opened a photographic studio on Cross Street in the 1850s. By the following decade James Mudd had a studio in St Ann's Square. His son later joined the business. James Mudd photographed scenes around Manchester, as he did locomotives built at the Beyer, Peacock works at Gorton. Mudd took some of the photographs in Section 1 of this book: Nineteenth Century.

Two Manchester photographers who worked during both the Victorian and Edwardian years were Warwick Brookes and Robert Banks. Brookes had a portrait studio on Oxford Road. His cousin, also called Warwick Brookes, was a local photographer too. This caused the Warwick Brookes of Oxford Road to put notices on the reverse of his portraits, disclaiming any business association with the other photographer of the same name. As well as studio portraits, Brookes (of Oxford Road) photographed the newly built Midland Hotel around 1903 and the Royal Infirmary, also when newly built. The infirmary, ready by 1908, was just across the road from the Oxford Road studio. Robert Banks photographed scenes in Manchester and beyond. He produced studio portraits and images of streets, local events, the Manchester Ship Canal and the Whit Walks. In 1893, Banks was at the Fallowfield Stadium to capture a scene from the FA Cup final that year between Wolverhampton Wanderers and Everton.

By the early years of the twentieth century, photographic depictions of towns and cities were available through the medium of the picture postcard. These have survived in great numbers and examples are reproduced in this book. Publishers of these cards ranged in size of operation from major national companies, producing their postcards on a factory scale using mechanised processes, down to local photographers printing their work in a more personal and hands-on way.

Instances of such local photographers include Berne Lancelot Pearson, who was the son of a butcher from Ardwick. Pearson was a self-employed photographer by the age of sixteen and worked from Ardwick, then later at his studio on Oldham Road in Newton Heath. Edward Vincent Ward was the son of a photographer and dealer in microscopes and slides. The father, also called Edward, had a shop on Oxford Road, near Owens College, which later became Manchester University. Edward Ward Jr took over the shop and followed his father as a photographer, producing postcard photographs of staff and students at the university, and of soldiers in military hospitals during the First World War. Another cameraman active before and during the First World War was John Cleworth. He was a leading Manchester pharmacist from Greenheys who, like Ward, also photographed students and military subjects. It was said in a 1931 pharmacy trade journal that, before newspapers carried many photographs, Cleworth put prints in his windows of events that had occurred earlier the same day.

William Edward Stansfeld Parker specialised in school photography after military service during the First World War. His father had been a solicitor in Wales but, after bankruptcy, moved his family to Salford where he was a greengrocer. The son had worked as a grocer until the war when he joined the Manchester Regiment. After the war he took a course in photography and started a business in which he visited schools in the Manchester area, taking class portraits for purchase as photographic postcards. Another interwar local photographer producing images in postcard format was Arthur Harold Clarke from Chorlton-cum-Hardy. He was active in the 1930s, capturing views of Manchester streets and buildings.

This book, an annotated pictorial album of Manchester, offers a selection of the many photographs made of the city and includes images from the nineteenth century until well into the twentieth. While some of the photographers can be named, others remain unidentified.

Section 1

Nineteenth Century

Market Place, 1859. By the middle decades of the nineteenth century photographic studios were a well-established feature of town and city life. This view is credited to James Mudd, one of Manchester's leading practitioners. The Wellington Inn is seen on the right, with the giant spectacles serving as a sign that the premises were also occupied by an optician called T. M. Bowen, advertised in 1863 as an 'Optical and Mathematical Instrument Maker'. Seen ahead is the rounded end of the then Royal Exchange building, on the corner of Market Street and Exchange Street.

The Exchange, designed by Thomas Harrison and built 1806–09. Before the advent of photography, depictions of people and places depended on the skill of artists and engravers. This image is typical of a topographical engraving from the pre-photography age. The semicircular end was used as a subscription library. Exchange Street, St Ann's Square and St Ann's Church are also seen.

New portico of the Exchange. In the 1840s, local architect Alexander Mills was commissioned to increase the capacity of Harrison's building. The portico fronts what was then called Bank Street (not the present Old Bank Street), built over during the major enlargement of 1914–21. In 1849, when the works had been completed, a grand ball was held to mark the opening, with funds going to local baths and washhouses.

Newall's Buildings on the corner of Cross Street and Market Street. The building is seen here not long before its demolition for another extension to the Royal Exchange, resulting in the 1874 building of Mills & Murgatroyd. In the 1840s, this had been the nerve centre of the Anti-Corn-Law League, a national campaign to end the levying of tariffs on imported grain. Local politician Richard Cobden was a key activist in this movement. The League occupied most of the building from where, according to one contemporary account, 'letters to the amount of several thousands a day go forth to all parts of the United Kingdom'.

St Ann's Church seen in 1863. It was built for Lady Ann Bland, born to the Mosley family, then Lords of the Manor of Manchester, and was consecrated in 1712. The church was a politico-religious reaction to the then type of worship at the Collegiate Church (now cathedral), seen as high Tory. Cobden's statue, unveiled in 1867, had yet to appear in St Ann's Square at the date of the photograph.

View from Blackfriars Bridge in 1859. It gives an idea of the then industrial activity on the banks of the River Irwell. Louis M. Hayes, a Manchester oil merchant, in his 1905 book looking back over the previous sixty years, wrote that the cathedral had, as long as he could recall, been in the 'hands of architects, builders and masons'. He also noted that passages from Deansgate led to riverside warehouses. The cathedral tower, seen in the distance, had not yet been rebuilt (work undertaken in the 1860s). Victoria Bridge, replacing the Salford Old Bridge, had opened with some ceremony in 1839.

Victoria Street in 1860. This section was built over during redevelopment in the 1970s. That has also been replaced with post-1996 rebuilding. Travelling down the road in the image would have brought you to the cathedral. The building on the right, end on to the street, was a fish market and opened in 1828. The other end of this market abutted onto the Market Place. This fish market was demolished during the nineteenth century and replaced by a building that became the Coal Exchange, itself destroyed during the Second World War.

Vintners' Arms on an old and narrow street called Smithy Door. The photograph is dated 1865 and shows the Vintners' Arms before it and all around was demolished for an imposing 1870s development called the Victoria Buildings, which was itself destroyed in the Second World War. Victoria Buildings (and the Vintners' Arms before it) stood between the lost part of Victoria Street and Deansgate.

This photograph is from ten years later. The Vintners' Arms and its egg, fish and butter-dealing neighbour at 7 Smithy Door are awaiting their fate. In 1863, when Smithy Door was still a living street, the trade directory records businesses selling not only foodstuffs, but also a clockmaker, tailor and fire engine manufacturer.

Main post office on Brown Street. The photograph dates from the 1870s. A new, grander post office was built the following decade, with its principal entrance on Spring Gardens instead of Brown Street. The building seen here was demolished for the rebuild. It had been opened in 1840 and was owned by Sir Oswald Mosley, Lord of the Manor of Manchester. The upper part of the building was used as the borough court.

The former Town Hall, King Street, in 1875. The Waterhouse-designed building in Albert Square would be formally opened two years later. This earlier Town Hall was built for a body called the Police Commissioners, who acted with certain local government powers, including street lighting and improvements, and they provided a night watch. They were not elected but served through property or other qualifications. The foundation stone was laid in 1822 and the building was ready three years later. After Manchester's first council was elected in 1838, it was at first denied use of this building by the rival commissioners. Instead they met in the York Hotel, seen on the right of the frame.

James Mudd, photographer, who made several of the studies in this section of the book. The image reproduced here shows the back of a studio portrait credited to James Mudd & Son (his son, James Willis Mudd, had joined his father's business by the 1870s). The ornate style might reflect the fact that Mudd Snr had been a textile pattern designer. The studio was in St Ann's Square, a sought-after trade address. James Mudd also did work for Beyer, Peacock of Gorton, photographing newly built locomotives.

Exhibition of Art Treasures of the United Kingdom. This was located at Old Trafford, away from the central area and its industrial atmosphere. The organisers had feared that any risk of damage to art works by pollution may have deterred owners from lending from their collections. The place chosen for the temporary exhibition buildings was on land next to the botanical gardens. The Manchester Cricket Club was paid to surrender its lease and moved to the site of the present Lancashire ground. The exhibition was opened by Prince Albert in May 1857 (Victoria came in June) and was visited by 1.3 million people. It closed in October the same year.

FA Cup final, 1893. This retouched photograph was taken by Robert Banks at the Fallowfield Stadium, home of the Manchester Athletic Club. It shows a back-of-the-crowd scene from the match between Wolverhampton Wanderers and Everton, a contest won 1-0 by Wolves. Fans, described as 'country cousins', had arrived by 'excursion trains from places near and far' and made their way along Oxford Road and Wilmslow Road on foot, by tram or omnibus. The numbers appeared to overwhelm the venue, with Everton later complaining to the FA about spectators up to the touchline affecting their game.

Robert Banks, Manchester photographer. He worked during the later Victorian years and into the twentieth century. Three of his studio addresses are shown on the back of this so-called *carte de visite*, popular from the 1850s to the end of the century. These were small photographs stuck on a card backing, which could be used by the photographer, as here, for advertising and self-promotion. Banks did studio portrait work, but also photographed buildings, street scenes and newsworthy events.

ST. PATRICK'S CHURCH, LIVSEY STREET, MANCHESTER.

Lancashire. No. 953.

St Patrick's, Livesey Street, Collyhurst. This first building of 1832 was described as being a 'square cruciform church ... with galleries'. The Roman Catholic parish, which included Failsworth, Harpurhey and Blackley, numbered 30,000 in 1835. The church seen here was demolished and a new building erected, which opened in 1937. This *carte de visite* image by a German-born Manchester photographer, Helmut Petschler, is from the 1860s.

Helmut Petschler 1863 trade directory advert. By the 1860s, photographic studios and suppliers were well established in most urban centres. Manchester was no exception. Petschler moved from Germany to Manchester, where there was a large German community. He photographed topographical views not only of Manchester, but also in other northern locations. With his English wife, also a photographer, they formed the Manchester Photographic Company in 1865, although this soon went into liquidation. He died in 1869.

Section 2

City Centre

Manchester Cathedral, a typical postcard photograph. Most of the images that follow in this and subsequent sections are from the twentieth century. A bountiful source from this period was the vintage picture postcard. Postcard publishers from the first half of the century issued many cards that were real photographs, rather than ink-printed by one technique or another. The dating of postcards, though, can be problematic as images were sometimes used again on later issues and so posting dates may be deceptive.

View from Victoria Buildings, which stood at the angle of Deansgate and a former part of Victoria Street. The upper storeys offered a camera position that enabled photographs such as this from the early 1930s. As well as the cathedral, the frame captures Exchange station on the Salford side of the Irwell, and the Cromwell statue, unveiled in 1875. In the 1960s, Exchange station was closed to passenger traffic and Cromwell was moved to improve traffic flows.

The garden seen in this 1950s view gives an idea of the triangular footprint of the war-destroyed Victoria Buildings. The Cromwell statue can just be made out beyond the apex of the garden. On the right is a part of Victoria Street that was built over in a 1970s development. The buildings on the left, also long gone, included the Deansgate Hotel and at the end was another hotel, the Grosvenor.

The Old Wellington Inn and Sinclair's Oyster Bar. They are seen here in the historic Market Place after the Second World War, when the use of bomb sites as car parks is evident. They give an idea of Manchester buildings before the industrial age. John Byrom, son of a linen draper, was born in 1691 at what later became the Wellington Inn. He invented a shorthand system, and wrote the hymn 'Christians Awake'. In the 1970s, the ancient buildings were raised around 5 feet as part of a development that placed them in a new space called Shambles Square. Following the 1996 bomb, they were relocated and reconfigured.

The Seven Stars on Withy Grove. This was a popular subject in the early 1900s for those wanting to depict a pictorial view of a lost and bygone Manchester. The inn, seen here flanked by unprepossessing commercial buildings, was alive with history – real and fictional. Local novelist Harrison Ainsworth had Guy Fawkes take refuge at the Seven Stars. Despite protests, it was demolished in 1911.

Poet's Corner on Long Millgate. This was another of those ancient buildings that the nineteenth-century industrial and commercial tide had not swept away. It had been a hostelry called the Sun Inn, and a poetry group met here, hence the popular name. In this photograph it is an antiques shop. It stood on a bend in the road, across from Chetham's Hospital and Manchester Grammar School, then also on Long Millgate. It was demolished in 1923.

Poet's Corner from the opposite direction to that in the previous image. The narrowness of Long Millgate is shown, as is the bend in the road. In the background one of the Manchester Grammar School buildings can be seen, which has survived as part of Chetham's music school. It was linked by a bridge to another grammar school building, which was off frame to the right.

The Royal Exchange. Seen here on the corner of Cross Street and Market Street, it was the trading hub of the Lancashire textile industry. It was completed in 1874, replacing an earlier Royal Exchange on part of the same site. In order that this building could extend to Cross Street, other properties were demolished. This included Newall's Buildings, the one-time head office of the Anti-Corn-Law League, which stood on this corner.

The Corn Exchange. This was just a short walk away from the Royal Exchange and provided Manchester and the region with various wholesale food provisions. There had been an earlier Corn Exchange, built in 1837, but the need for enlargement created the building seen here. It was built between 1891 and 1903. The photograph shows the Corn Exchange around the time of its completion in the early 1900s.

The Assize Courts. The building was situated in front of the prison at Strangeways and opened in 1864. Alfred Waterhouse had won the design competition, although his plans were not without criticism. He had placed female witness rooms next to public toilets! The building was erected on the site of Strangeways Hall, with work commencing in 1859. Bombed during the Second World War, the edifice was almost destroyed. Cecil Stewart, in his 1956 *Stones of Manchester*, called it a 'very impressive ruin'.

Female warders at Strangeways Prison. The photograph was taken in 1911, a time when there was major industrial action, and the civil disobedience campaign for women's suffrage was also causing problems for the authorities. At this time, the prison was for both men and women. It had been designed by Alfred Waterhouse and opened in 1868, replacing the New Bailey in Salford.

BOROUGH & COUNTY POLICE. MANCHESTER LABOUR DISPUTE 1911.

Local police augmented by county officers, 1911. The years before the First World War saw a militancy among certain sections of workers. For example, those employed in key jobs for the handling and distribution of foodstuffs caused alarm when they went on strike. The year 1911 was one of major unrest, with local dockers and carters withdrawing their labour. The carters' strike over union recognition and improved conditions affected food distribution, with police protecting those still working. The photograph was taken by Berne Lancelot Pearson, who had a studio on Oldham Road, Newton Heath.

Winston Churchill. For much of 1911, Churchill was the Home Secretary, with responsibility for the police. He had represented Oldham from 1900, at first as a Conservative before joining the Liberals. In the 1906 general election he won the then seat of Manchester North West for the Liberal Party. On promotion to the Cabinet, the rules at the time forced him to stand in a by-election in 1908. He lost to his Conservative opponent, William Joynson-Hicks.

21

Deansgate. In 1876, the *Graphic*, an illustrated journal, ran a special feature on Manchester. It stated that in the 1860s Deansgate was a 'narrow, dirty lane'. However, by the date of publication it had become 'one of the handsomest thoroughfares in England'. This was due to street improvements and widening following a parliamentary Act of 1869. Old buildings were pulled down and major new architecture appeared. This photograph shows what are now lost buildings of the 1870s, including, nearer the camera, an entrance to the one-time Exchange Arcade, and beyond St Mary's Gate, the Victoria Buildings.

Deansgate junction with St Mary's Street. The corner building had the London, City & Midland Bank at street level, but above was the photographic studio of Lafayette Ltd. Some of the sign lettering can be made out. Despite its French-sounding name, this company had been founded in Dublin by a James Lauder. Studios were opened in Glasgow, London and Belfast, as well as Manchester. The building was called Arcade Chambers.

Deansgate in the early 1930s, with the camera pointing northwards. The light-coloured building with the tower was Northcliffe House, home of Associated Newspapers who published the *Daily Mail*. Around the time of the photograph it was a rebuild of an earlier building for the same newspaper, which was also on the corner of Deansgate and Hardman Street. It was demolished in 2002. Offices of the Inland Revenue are on the left, and opposite, those of the Manchester Education Committee.

Milton Hall, Deansgate. The building was erected on the west side of Deansgate around 1911, on a site given by Mrs Rylands. It was also called Congregational Church House. John Rylands had been a Congregationalist. Quay Street is off frame to the right. This photograph gives an idea of earlier buildings on Deansgate, which are seen flanking the Edwardian newcomer.

23

Market Place, probably 1920s. The advent of motor vehicles is certainly evident. This location had been the hub of medieval Manchester, although by the twentieth century the street stalls had been removed. The cathedral is in the distance and the Royal Exchange is a little way behind the photographer. The centuries-old Wellington Inn is shielded by taller buildings. This helped it survive the worst of the bombing, when much here was destroyed in the Second World War. Development in the 1970s completed the effacement.

St Mary's Gate, around 1910. Wyman's were a company that ran railway station bookstalls. They also produced picture postcards. This is a real photograph issued as a Wyman's Series postcard. The viewer is looking down St Mary's Gate to the Deansgate junction. On the left is Exchange Street, and on the right, a former section of Victoria Street. The war-destroyed Victoria Buildings stand on the right.

St Ann's Square, early 1900s. It takes its name from the church, consecrated in 1712. The building of the church saw the former Acres Field become a fashionable eighteenth-century location. It was residential at first, but in the nineteenth century shops and other commercial interests appeared. Cabs, horse-drawn in this photograph, had plied from the square from 1810. Photographers such as James Mudd opened studios in here.

St Ann's Square, mid-1920s. The former equine cabs have been replaced by a line of motorised taxis. On the left, the nearest parked car is outside the premises of William Arnold, a Bentley dealer. The Royal Exchange had been extended into the square by 1921, and on the right, the light-coloured building had been recently opened for Manchester Liners, whose vessels sailed from Salford Docks.

Royal Exchange postcard mailed from Manchester to France in 1912. The reason that the sender has written on the front was to comply with postal regulations in certain countries. The address had to be on the other side, without any message. This no longer applied to internal UK postcards. The view shows the Royal Exchange before it was extended into St Ann's Square during the enlargement of 1914–21. Prior to this it went only as far as the former Bank Street, seen here beyond the nearest cab.

St Ann's Square, 1920s. The image gives an idea of how the Royal Exchange was carried into the square, giving a greater length to the building and increased floor space inside. Scaffolding is also noted on the right, where the Manchester Liners building is still under construction.

St Ann's Square from the church. The church offered a useful vantage point for photographers seeking a high angle shot. This overview was taken around 1932. The photograph reveals the increased use of motor vehicles. The taxis are still lined up down the centre, but there are a significant number of parked cars.

St Ann's Square, around 1960. The cars and taxis are of their time, and the square is still far from traffic-free. A new building has appeared, seen across on the left. It was built at large expense in the late 1950s for the Royal Insurance Company. Here it is new and pristine. Cobden's statue surveys the then modern world.

Market Street, early 1900s. The street was once known as Market Stead Lane. As its name suggests, it led to the old Market Place. Until the nineteenth century it was narrow and crooked, sloping downhill. In 1821, special commissioners were appointed to oversee its improvement under an Act of that year. This view shows the junction with Cross Street, where electric trams are running along this street and Corporation Street, but Market Street still has horse power.

Market Street from the junction with Cross Street. The tram is turning into Market Street en route to Palatine Road from Albert Square. Manchester's first electrified tram route was inaugurated in 1901, and the following year Market Street was ready for electric trams. However, not everyone was happy with the new trams. The Horse Owners Union complained about the problems caused to horse-drawn vehicles by the innovation.

Market Street between Cross Street and St Mary's Gate, around 1910. This is another of the Wyman's Series postcards. It looks as if the photograph was taken from the open balcony of a tram. On the left is the Royal Exchange, not long before it was rebuilt and enlarged. In the distance are the Victoria Buildings. On the right, the buildings accommodated various shops and businesses, including, according to the 1911 directory, the *Liverpool Daily Post* and *Liverpool Echo* branch offices.

The Piccadilly end of Market Street in Edwardian times. High Street is just out of frame to the right. The view shows the site of the later Arndale Centre, so all these buildings have been demolished. They are varied in architecture and individualistic. Hope Brothers were hosiers and outfitters. In the buildings, above the street-level shops, were a multiplicity of businesses – agents, merchants and accountants among others.

Market Street, mid-1920s. The traffic gives a period feel to the scene, and the Royal Exchange tower orientates the viewer. The buildings on the right gave themselves over to the Arndale Centre. On the other side is the Clarion Café. This was a meeting place for young socialists, who possibly read the *Clarion* newspaper. They came to discuss political matters or just to meet up. Vegetarian meals were on the menu. It closed in 1936.

Market Street, possibly early 1950s. The shoppers are out in numbers but rationing was still then a fact of life. One big difference to the street from before the war was that the trams had gone. The 1950s also saw Rylands become Paulden's, a store from Chorlton-on-Medlock that was gutted by fire in 1957 and moved to the Market Street building.

Cross Street by South King Street. The name appears on Laurent's map of 1795, although it only formed part of the present street. There was also a Red Cross Street and, between Chapel Walks and Market Street, a Pool Fould (Fold). Around 1828, these were straightened and widened, and given the modern name for the whole length. On the left is Eagle Star House, built in 1911, around the date of the photograph. The end part of the former Town Hall, here a library, is seen on the right at King Street.

Cross Street, early 1930s. Seen in the middle distance on the right, at the King Street corner, is the light-coloured Portland stone, baroque-style bank building that had replaced the one-time Town Hall in 1915. On Cross Street at this time, out of camera view, were the offices of the *Manchester Guardian*. Facing the newspaper building was the Royal Exchange.

Albert Square, early 1900s. Writing in 1878, one observer recalled that twenty years before, the site had been 'intersected by narrow dirty streets and gloomy alleys, with dingy-looking dwellings'. Following the death of Prince Albert in 1861, Manchester decided to erect a memorial. Although Piccadilly had been suggested as a location, the 'dingy-looking' buildings were cleared away from this area for the new Albert Square. The memorial was formally presented to the city in 1867. Others statues followed: Bishop Fraser, John Bright, Oliver Heywood and William Gladstone. The spider's web of overhead wires confirms that electric trams were in service by the early 1900s.

Manchester Town Hall, around 1963. Construction lasted from 1868 to 1877, when it was formally opened. The building was designed by Alfred Waterhouse. The front, facing Albert Square, is not the longest side; the Princess Street and Lloyd Street elevations are longer. In 1963, joyous scenes were enacted here when Manchester United returned with the FA Cup, Matt Busby's first major trophy after the Munich air crash.

Aerial view from the 1930s overlooking Albert and St Peter's Squares. The Town Hall Extension is light and pristine. Along with Midland Hotel, it encloses the rounded form of the Central Library. At the bottom left corner is the arched roof of Central station with its covered walkway to the hotel. Oxford Street runs down towards the bottom of the frame on the right. The light-coloured building fronting the street was the Paramount (later Odeon) cinema. It opened in 1930, but has now been demolished.

Mount Street, around 1950. The two civic buildings of the 1930s – the Central Library and Town Hall Extension – were conceived as a composite design by Emanuel Vincent Harris, although stylistically different. Here they have had more than a decade's worth of weathering. At this time, Manchester Corporation was a municipal supplier of gas and electricity, and kitchen showrooms were found in the Town Hall Extension.

St Peter's Church, around 1906. Designed by James Wyatt, who also worked on Heaton Hall, it was consecrated in 1794. At the time, it was on the edge of town and Oxford Street hardly existed. The first rector, Samuel Hall, was a one-time tutor of Thomas de Quincey, who wrote about St Peter's. Hall had been a curate at St Ann's Church, and St Peter's was built for him by subscribers and wealthy supporters after he failed to secure a position at the Collegiate Church.

St Peter's Church interior during demolition. The church had been built to help meet the needs of an increasing population. It gave the name to nearby St Peter's Field where, in 1819, the Peterloo Massacre had taken place. Because of its musical recitals, it was said to attract 'fashionable idlers of the town'. When St Peter's was demolished, the organ, once the largest in England, was moved to St Bride's Church, Old Trafford. By the twentieth century, there were too few parishioners and the church closed in 1906. It was demolished by the next year.

Cleared site of St Peter's Church. The Midland Hotel, looming in the background, was just a few years old at the date of the photograph. On the ground where the Central Library was built in the 1930s, are buildings that contained offices for various trades and businesses. At street level was the 'Metro Smoking Café, Miss Mary Barnes, proprietress'.

St Peter's Church memorial cross in around 1908. This was the year the cross was dedicated. In 1924, it was joined by the cenotaph. Later, there was a memorial garden. During Metrolink tram works the cross was removed, then brought back and rededicated in 2017 by the Bishop of Manchester, David Walker.

St Peter's Square postcard from around 1953. It gives an idea of the then traffic island setting of the St Peter's cross, cenotaph and garden. Opposite are buildings that were demolished for Elizabeth House, now itself demolished. These buildings have a Hallé Concerts shop at street level, not far from the Free Trade Hall on Peter Street.

Lloyd Street, 1940s. When Vincent Harris designed the Town Hall Extension, he opted to link his own 1930s building (on the left) with Alfred Waterhouse's 1877 Town Hall, using these two bronze-fronted bridges.

The Free Trade Hall, early 1900s. The building was opened in 1856, replacing a brick-built hall of 1843. This earlier building was a meeting place for anti-Corn Law activists, hence the name. The site of these buildings had been St Peter's Field, where the killings of 1819 had taken place. As well as political meetings, the hall in the photograph was once the venue for the Hallé concerts. Rebuilt after wartime bombing, it later became a hotel.

Mosley Street by Princess Street. The character of the street changed during the nineteenth century, when homes of the affluent became warehouses and commercial interests took over. It was not all business though. The Manchester City Art Gallery, seen here, was in a building designed by Charles Barry, who later worked on the Houses of Parliament. This had been built for the Royal Manchester Institution, which promoted the arts, literature and science. Beyond the gallery is the Union Club, which in 1876 was said to be 'housed in a building which would do no discredit to Pall Mall'.

The Midland Hotel from Lower Mosley Street. The hotel was opened in 1903 for the Midland Railway, which worked its trains from Central station. It was Manchester's most luxurious hotel where Rolls and Royce famously met. There was a covered walkway from the station to this Windmill Street entrance to the hotel.

Midland Hotel interior view. The hotel had been designed by the Midland Railway's own architect, Charles Trubshaw. The external materials were granite, brick and terracotta. The Gentlemen's Concert Hall had been demolished for the hotel, which was then replaced by a hotel theatre. There were also a palm court, winter gardens and roof garden. This early image was taken by an Oxford Road photographer, Warwick Brookes, who also photographed the Royal Infirmary when new.

View from the Central Library, 1930s. Oxford Street, which becomes Oxford Road and Wilmslow Road, runs down past the railway bridge to the university, hospitals and on to the southern suburbs. Below are the cenotaph and St Peter's cross. On the right, the corner buildings were replaced in the late 1950s by Peter House. The lighter building was the Prince's Theatre, which closed in 1940 and was demolished. Further down the street, on the left, was the Paramount (later Odeon) cinema of 1930, whose long auditorium roof can be seen. This has also now gone.

An Edwardian view of Oxford Street. In this photograph, the camera is by the Palace Theatre, which opened on Oxford Street in 1891. Further on, the building with the clock tower was the St James's Hall. This had opened in 1881 as a venue for concerts, public meetings and other events. There was also a theatre with its own entrance. In 1901, a fundraising bazaar was held here for the cash-strapped Newton Heath football club. The following year they changed their name to Manchester United.

St James's Building, Oxford Street. The St James's Hall and Theatre were demolished for a Portland stone giant, the St James's Buildings. It was built in 1912 for a textile grouping called the Calico Printers' Association. Beyond, on the Whitworth Street corner, rises the clock tower of the then Refuge Assurance building. The tower was not an original feature, but added when the 1890s building was extended in 1910–12.

Oxford Street at the junction with Whitworth Street. The tramways at this location had not yet been converted to electric power, which was introduced by the end of 1902. There is a good view of the Palace Theatre, then further along, the St James's Hall clock tower. In the far distance, the St Peter's Church tower can just be seen.

St Mary's Hospital, Whitworth Street West. This photographic postcard was issued by James L. Brown, a local card publisher active during the interwar years. The hospital has a history dating back to 1790, when it was first founded for female patients. Several relocations led to this site being purchased in 1890 on what was then called Gloucester Street. Oxford Street is on the right. The building was designed by Waterhouse & Son and had opened by 1904. It closed in 1969 and was subsequently demolished.

Piccadilly in the early twentieth century. The Victoria statue, unveiled in 1901, is in place. The nearest statue, Wellington, dating from 1856, was by Matthew Noble, who also produced the Prince Albert work in Albert Square. The Lewis's tower is in the distance. Out of shot on the left was the old infirmary.

Royal Infirmary, Piccadilly. The infirmary had started in 1752 at a house in Garden Street, off Shudehill. It then moved to land acquired from Oswald Mosley, lord of the manor, opening in 1755. Additions made that same century include baths, a dispensary and what was termed a 'lunatic asylum'. The architectural style was due to work in the mid-nineteenth century, supervised by local architect Richard Lane. It closed in 1908 and was demolished two years later. Manchester Corporation purchased the Piccadilly site, giving them a large open space in the centre of the city.

Postcard view of Piccadilly in the early 1930s. On the left are the huts that served as a reference library before the new Central Library was built. The then new Rylands warehouse (later Paulden's, then Debenhams) is in the distance.

Piccadilly, 1950s. The gardens and lawns had been laid out on the old infirmary site by the 1920s. Directly across, on Portland Street, are darkened warehouse buildings and, next to them, the lighter Queen's Hotel. The row on the left includes the former Woolworth's store and, next but one, the taller building that was then the regional BBC centre.

Oldham Street before the First World War. It was then a major shopping location. The street was named after an eighteenth-century Methodist, Adam Oldham. The photographer is aiming the camera northwards, with Piccadilly behind. The nearest roundel sign on the right is for Annie Harrison's servants' registry, an address she shared with a palmist, Madame Ricardo. Just beyond was a Woolworth's branch. Past Hilton Street, on the same side, was Abel Heywood & Son's bookshop.

Oldham Street looking south, in the direction of Piccadilly. On the left is the ornate store front of Boots Cash Chemist. The junction at the end of the block is with Hilton Street. The corner building with the dome advertises itself as a mourning warehouse. The tram is heading to Clayton.

Section 3

Business, Trade and Industry

Potato merchants, Smithfield Market. Working Manchester embraced many activities, from worldwide trading on the floor of the Royal Exchange to stallholders trying to make a living on a street market. The city not only sold and dealt, but also manufactured. The images throughout this section depict some of this.

George Allen, photographer and provider of equipment and supplies. The shop, seen here in the 1920s, was on Oldham Road. His neighbour sold records and radios. Allen later moved to other premises on the same road, closer to the city centre. His advertising was then able to claim he was only seven minutes from Piccadilly.

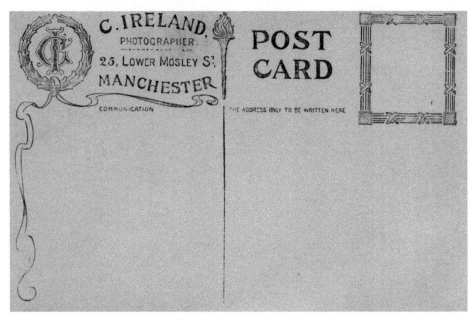

Photographer Charles Ireland, advertising his business on the back of a postcard. The Victorians had used the backing board of so-called *carte de visite* photographs to promote themselves. In the twentieth century, when postcard stationery became available as a photographic print medium, photographers often used a simple name and address. The one reproduced here is a little more eye-catching.

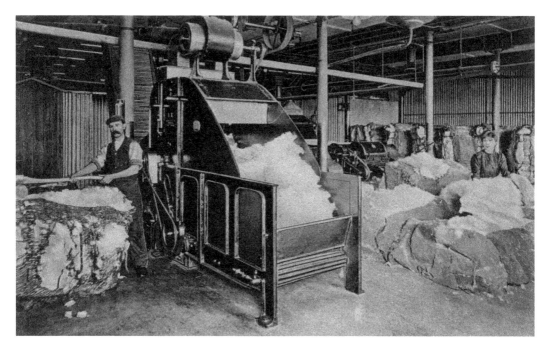

Cotton processing on a postcard. The card was used as advertising by textile manufacturer Richard Haworth & Co., who had cotton mills in Salford and a Manchester warehouse on Dale Street. By the mid-nineteenth century, Manchester had become a city of warehouses and exchange, rather than one of production.

The Royal Exchange, around 1922. The view is from St Ann's Square, and the photograph was taken shortly after the building was extended. It had been formally opened in 1921 by George V. The lighter building to the right, still under construction, was for Manchester Liners, a shipping company that played its own role in the region's trading.

The Royal Exchange interior around 1922. A 1940s Manchester guide called it the 'Heart of Lancashire' and 'one of the sights of Britain'. When trade was good, several thousand would assemble on this floor. For members, there were a reading room and large number of telephone lines. Renovation after wartime bombing reduced the floor area.

The Royal Exchange on a business day. These apparently chaotic scenes, with thousands of traders on the floor at once, look like an impossible situation to navigate. However, the regular dealers knew where to find who they needed to meet. There were cotton spinners and brokers, yarn agents, bleachers, engineers, and merchants in iron, steel, leather and oil. These busy times of get-together were called High Change. Trading ceased in 1968.

The Coal Exchange at the old Market Place. The Royal Exchange was not Manchester's only trading market. This scene shows a crowd gathered near the building to the right of the Wellington Inn. This was the Coal Exchange, built on the site of the former fish market. These people would have been traders. As well as coal interests, the building was also an exchange for cotton waste dealers. It was destroyed in the Second World War.

The Corn Exchange, Hanging Ditch, around 1910. An earlier Corn Exchange, designed by Richard Lane, was opened in 1837. An 1850 guide admired its architecture, but wrote that until the then new Corporation Street was completed, it would not be seen to advantage. Fifty years or so later, the Corn & Produce Exchange seen in the photograph had replaced it, and could be viewed to visual effect.

Co-operative Wholesale Society buildings, Corporation Street. The northern end of this street became home to the Co-operative movement. The two buildings in the photograph are almost twins, separated by Balloon Street, the official address. The CWS supplied a range of goods to local Co-operative societies for their retail stores. It also manufactured its own products in CWS factories. There was a CWS biscuit factory at Crumpsall. The nearer building was demolished for the 1970s Co-op Bank.

Manchester & Salford Equitable Co-operative Society in the interwar period. This was a typical Co-operative society. It originated in 1858 at Roby Sunday School. Enough members were found to open a shop on Great Ancoats Street. Other shops were opened, including one in Salford. The headquarters were established in Downing Street, Ardwick. As well as selling goods, education was part of the Co-operative ethos, and there was a library at Downing Street. Mergers with other societies saw the Manchester & Salford lose its separate identity.

Trade card for S. & J. Watts, posted in 1938. The business was a major home trade wholesale draper, and opened a huge and ornate warehouse in 1858, on Portland Street. The card shows that the Watts family were still in charge in the 1930s. This was sent to a company in Lowestoft, presumably arranging an appointment. After threat of demolition, the building was converted to a hotel in the 1980s.

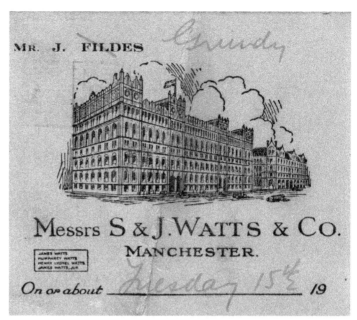

MR. J. FILDES

Messrs S & J. WATTS & CO.
MANCHESTER.

On or about _____ 19

Rylands warehouse from Market Street. John Rylands was born in St Helens and, with his father and brothers, established a textile business in Wigan. A warehouse was opened in Manchester, which suffered major fire damage in 1854. The 1863 directory gives the buildings as along High Street and the company listed as manufacturers, warehousemen and merchants. The photograph shows Rylands & Sons in the twentieth century. The nearest corner is Tib Street, with High Street at the end of the block.

51

Rylands, Market Street, around 1950. The former Rylands warehouse was demolished for a new, Portland stone building, completed in 1932. Around the date of the photograph, the interior, with its 'spacious display features', was considered to be as 'striking as its geometric exterior'. Paulden's, a department store from Chorlton-on-Medlock, later owned by Debenhams, moved in after its own store was destroyed by fire in 1957. The Rylands building became known as Paulden's, then Debenhams.

Lewis's on the corner of Market Street and Fountain Street. Lewis's was an iconic Manchester department store that opened in 1880. It was not strictly a local store, as the group started in Liverpool and there were branches in other cities. The first building was smaller than the one seen here and had a clock tower. There was a rebuild in 1915, then an extension in 1929. The picture was by local photographer Arthur Harold Clarke, from Chorlton-cum-Hardy, who documented the city in the 1930s.

Affleck & Brown's drapery store around 1905. This Oldham Street store has been photographed at the junction with Church Street, on the left. It occupied the block to Hilton Street, and as far back as Tib Street. It was one of the main shopping attractions in what was once an important retail street. It remained a family-owned business until after the Second World War, before Debenhams acquired the building. It was later called the Smithfield Building, a residential conversion.

Kendal Milne store, Deansgate, possibly photographed in the 1950s. A long-established Manchester retailer, it had been owned by Harrods from 1919 until 1959, when House of Fraser bought it. However, the Kendal Milne name was retained until 2005. This building dates from 1940, but there were also departments across the road.

Fish stalls at the Market Place in the early twentieth century. Although the Market Place street stalls had gone by this time, these vendors are still selling in a narrow alleyway called Old Shambles. The Victoria Buildings, badly damaged in the Second World War, are in the background.

The hen market, Shudehill, seen in Edwardian days. This kerb market not only sold pets and poultry, but also became a popular place to browse second-hand books. The centuries-old Rover's Return that was demolished in the 1950s is in the background, as is the Old Mosley Arms pub, which was lost to the Arndale Centre.

Smithfield Market from a 1940s postcard. Oswald Mosley, lord of the manor, who then held the market rights, had established Smithfield by 1822. Manchester Corporation purchased Mosley's manorial rights, and the Markets Act of 1846 enabled it to control local markets. In 1854, Smithfield was roofed over in iron and glass. It served not only the city but also the wider region. The photograph gives an idea of the crates and boxes amid the wholesale trade in fruit and vegetables.

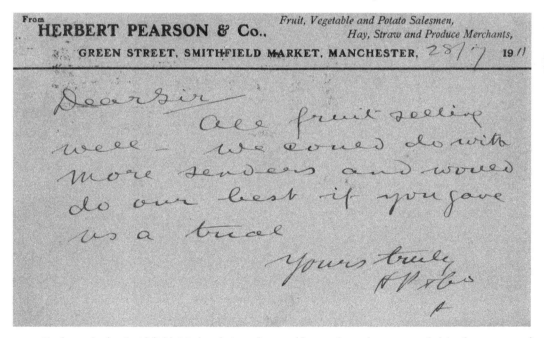

Trade card of a Smithfield Market fruit and vegetable merchant that was mailed in the summer of 1911. The card was posted to Cambridgeshire, stating that fruit was selling well and requesting to be supplied with more.

Mode Wheel Locks, Manchester Ship Canal, early twentieth century. The ship canal was a response to high dock charges at Liverpool and the cost of rail transportation. Despite political opposition and major engineering challenges, it opened in 1894. A tidal canal had been considered, but this was rejected in favour of a series of locks along the 35 miles of length to raise vessels to the level of the docks at the canal's head. Mode Wheel was the last of the locks before reaching the docks. The ship on the left is undergoing an inspection or repair in a floating dry dock.

The new Dock 9 in Edwardian times. The docks were numbered rather than named. The larger docks, Dock 6 to Dock 9, for ocean-going ships, were in Salford. The smaller docks, Dock 1 to Dock 4, for coastal shipping, lay mostly in Stretford and were known as 'Pomona Docks'. What was to be the largest of the docks, Dock 9, was built on the site of the former Manchester Racecourse (in Salford). It was ceremonially opened by Edward VII in July 1905. A planned Dock 10 was never constructed and Dock 5 was not completed, so there were eight docks in all.

The grain elevator, Trafford Wharf, Stretford, at work. The docks handled a range of goods, including imported raw materials, timber, oil and food. Finished products, including railway locomotives built in Manchester, were exported. The photograph shows the first grain elevator, which could discharge from ships at the rate of 350 tons per hour. A second was later built at the head of Dock 9.

Warehousing by Dock 9. Extensive and specialist storage facilities were required by the importers and exporters. The sheds seen here were built next to Dock 9, situated off frame to the left. On the right were railway marshalling yards. The Manchester Ship Canal Co. had its own railway system, which was linked to mainline networks.

An early view of the Westinghouse works, Trafford Park. The growth of Trafford Park, located close to the docks, created a huge industrial powerhouse for the region. The land had originally been owned by the de Trafford family, who sold it in 1896. One of the biggest employers was British Westinghouse, a subsidiary of the American company. In 1902, it began production of turbines and electric generators. There was also a company township for workers, laid out on the American grid system. Westinghouse later became Metropolitan-Vickers.

Winding department, Westinghouse. American firms brought their own production methods, notably Ford, which also established itself in Trafford Park before relocating to Dagenham. Westinghouse produced electric generators, transformers and motors, which required wire windings.

An exhibition of electrical appliances held at Platt Fields, 1908. Manchester had been generating its own electricity before 1900 and had an Electricity Committee. It was running electric trams by 1901. The exhibition was held in a temporary structure, with the Corporation installing an electric supply plant. Appropriately, after dark, the building was electrically illuminated.

Inside the electrical exhibition at Platt Fields, 1908. There was 100,000 square feet of floor space, with 65,000 given over to the stands of 250 exhibitors. One local name can be partly discerned high on the facing wall (the rest is hidden by foliage), that of Westinghouse.

Barton Power Station when newly built in the 1920s. Manchester Corporation had been a municipal supplier of electricity since the 1890s. It established a generating station at Dickenson Street in 1893, then another in Bloom Street. It took on the provision of lighting in several outer districts and, in order to meet demand, by 1902 had built a large station in Stuart Street, east Manchester. Barton power station was situated on the Bridgewater Canal, from where coal supplies came. It was demolished in the 1970s.

Plan for GAS

If you are one of the lucky ones, and are planning a new home, plan the fuel service in it, too. See that a gas point goes into every room. Ask us to help you design the kitchen, and let us give you facts and figures on gas for cooking, heating, water heating and refrigeration. That's the way, before a single brick is laid, to ensure a lifetime of domestic comfort, leisure and economy.

CITY OF MANCHESTER GAS DEPARTMENT
TOWN HALL, MANCHESTER, 2
Tel. Cen. 3377

A 1940s advertisement with 'Mr Therm', Manchester Corporation Gas Department. Manchester had been a provider of gas since 1843, when the Police Commissioners, who had been responsible for street lighting and other matters, handed over their gasworks. A century later, Manchester was still selling gas to its citizens.

Renold chain works, Burnage, between the wars. This company was founded by a Swiss immigrant, Hans Renold, who acquired a Salford chain-making firm in 1879. Expansion included building this factory at Burnage, which also made munitions during the First World War. The company has grown into a major manufacturer of gear and transmission systems. The buildings in the photograph have now been demolished.

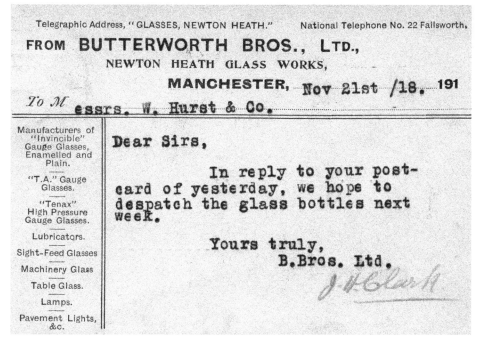

Glass manufacturer Newton Heath trade card from 1918. Manchester's varied manufacturing output is typified by this card, posted to notify about the imminent forwarding of glass bottles. The firm was based off Oldham Road, on Barker Street, which no longer exists.

EXCHANGE HOTEL, FENNEL STREET, MANCHESTER.

Commercial & Day Hotel and Restaurant.
Two minutes from Victoria and Exchange Stations
TELEGRAMS:
TELEPHONE NO. 164 CITY.   EXCHANGE HOTEL, MANCHESTER.

Exchange Hotel, Corn Exchange, Fennel Street. This hotel stood at the corner of Fennel Street, to the left, and Cathedral Street, on the right. It was part of the Corn Exchange building and this advertising card was probably aimed at wholesalers and buyers visiting Manchester for business.

"REEOS" COMPANY LTD.,
Shirt & Pyjama Manufacturers

Regent House, 30, Cannon Street, and 31, Tib Street, Manchester, 4.

DATE AS POSTMARK

Please note that after APRIL 20th 1950 our address will be :

PHOENIX MILLS,
PIERCY STREET,
ANCOATS,
MANCHESTER, 4.

Telephone : COLlyhurst 3425

A change of address card, 1950. This shirt and pyjama manufacturer is notifying of a new address in Ancoats, an early industrial suburb. With the decline of the cotton industry, other uses were found for one-time mills. Forty years before the firm's relocation, the Phoenix Mill had been home to firms involved in 'doubling', a textile process. Piercey Street, even then, had a shirt maker.

Section 4

Transport

Market Street, 1933. A large industrial and commercial conurbation such as Manchester was dependant on effective transport communications. The Bridgewater Canal was opened in the eighteenth century. During the following two centuries came the railways, motor-powered road vehicles and air transport. This view of Market Street, with Lewis's store in the background and a new H. Samuel branch on the right, shows a 1930s traffic scene.

Barton swing aqueduct, Manchester Ship Canal. When the Bridgewater Canal was constructed in the eighteenth century, one of its wonders was the stone-built aqueduct at Barton. This carried the new canal over the River Irwell. A swing aqueduct had replaced this when the Manchester Ship Canal was opened in 1894.

Barton swing aqueduct showing the sealed water trough, Manchester Ship Canal. The aqueduct at Barton, operational by 1893, was essentially an elongated water tank that could be temporarily sealed at both ends, then swung round to allow clear passage for shipping. This photograph shows the contained water, actually part of the Bridgewater Canal. The high-level towpath is noted on the left.

Mode Wheel Locks, Manchester Ship Canal, 1930s. The canal had been an attempt to reverse the economic decline of Manchester, seen as caused in part by Liverpool dock charges and rail costs incurred in the importing of food and raw materials, and exporting finished goods. Ships on the canal, which opened in 1894, were raised to Manchester's height above sea level by a series of locks. Mode Wheel Locks were the furthest from the Mersey estuary, and formed an entry to Manchester Docks. The viewpoint is towards the docks, located in the distance.

Rochdale Canal, Canal Street. The Rochdale Canal was ceremonially opened in 1804, when two boats brought company committee members from Rochdale to Manchester. There was also a military band. It traverses Manchester from the Piccadilly basin to the Bridgewater Canal at Castlefield. Connections with other canals made it part of a route between Liverpool and Hull. This view shows the waterway passing Canal Street on the left with cars and parking meters.

Victoria station, 1960s. The station opened in 1844 and was used by both the Liverpool & Manchester and Manchester & Leeds railways. The administration offices of the Lancashire & Yorkshire Railway (into which the M&LR had been absorbed) were later based here. The begrimed frontage, seen here in the 1960s, was due to a 1909 remodelling by local architect William Dawes.

Victoria station, around 1910. This Edwardian scene is from a time when Manchester was a vibrant commercial and industrial centre. Local commuters to the city (the districts Heywood, Bury and Middleton can be made out), and more distant travellers from the Lancashire coast and Yorkshire arrived here. Oldham's master cotton spinners, perhaps wearing bowler hats, would have come through on their way to the Royal Exchange.

Exchange station from Victoria Street, around 1910. This station had opened in 1884. It was built for the London & North Western Railway, which had previously shared Victoria's platforms with the Lancashire & Yorkshire Railway. The driveway, which spans the River Irwell, gave access to the station on the Salford side of the boundary. The prominent board advertising 'EXCURSIONS TO IRELAND', would possibly have been aimed at members of Manchester's large Irish population. Exchange closed in 1969.

London Road station (later Piccadilly) between the wars. This station had been built as a terminus for the Manchester & Birmingham Railway. The idea was to connect Manchester to the Midlands, and therefore to London. It opened in 1842. The Manchester & Birmingham Railway became part of the giant London & North Western Railway, then further restructuring in 1923 brought about the London Midland & Scottish grouping. This photograph was taken during LMS years, prior to rail nationalisation in the 1940s.

Central station, 1940s. The arched roof of Central station has been one of Manchester's eye-catching landmarks since 1880, when the station opened. The railway companies named on the building show that the photograph was taken before rail nationalisation in 1948. The bus says 'FORCES ONLY', and *Picture Post* was a photo-journalism publication issued between 1938 and 1957.

Manchester Collieries steam locomotive. This group of mines from the Manchester coalfield was formed in 1929. They were located in the wider Manchester region, with the headquarters in Walkden. The mines were interlinked by rail and also connected to mainline railways.

Hansom cab and electric tram, Deansgate, early 1900s. This photograph, perhaps set up, contrasts the old with the modern. The hansom cab, which spoke of the Victorian age, is side by side with the latest in transport modernism, the electric tram. The location is Deansgate. On the other side of the road is the corner with South King Street. The Percy sign was for jeweller and pawnbroker John Percy.

Tram on Route 28, near Piccadilly Gardens. The city's first trams were horse-hauled and run by a private company. In 1901, Manchester began operating its own fleet of electric trams. This tram is seen on a short section of George Street that no longer exists, but once extended to near Piccadilly Gardens. Route 28 ran to Ashton-under-Lyne via Ashton Old Road. The building in the background, on the left, was a warehouse on Parker Street, destroyed in the Second World War.

An illuminated tram for the royal visit in 1909. On special occasions trams were bedecked with lights and foliage. The tram in the photograph was decorated for the visit of Edward VII, who visited Manchester in July 1909 to ceremonially open the new Royal Infirmary. The image was by Berne Lancelot Pearson, a butcher's son from Ardwick, who was a self-employed photographer by the age of sixteen.

An illuminated tram for Civic Week, 1926. The week was intended to show its own citizens the work of local government, commerce and industry. They were invited to visit municipal buildings, factories and warehouses. In Heaton Park there was a historical pageant. It was also intended to boost the local economy by drawing the world's attention to Manchester's industrial capacity.

Traffic at the Portland Street and Oxford Street junction. Police on traffic duty at Manchester's city centre junctions and crossroads had a busy time of it. Portland Street, to the left, was home to large textile warehouses. Princess Street, which intersects Portland Street, also had warehouses. The empty steam lorry had probably just made a warehouse delivery. Trams added to the traffic mix.

Parker Street bus station, 1930s. When motor buses started to enter the city centre, it meant that Manchester needed a central bus station. Building on the Parker Street bus station commenced in 1931 and was completed a few years later. During the 1930s, there was a process of tram route abandonment in favour of buses.

Cabs and horse carriage, St Ann's Square. This location, convenient for exclusive shopping and the Royal Exchange, was one of the places from where cab fares were calculated. The four-wheeler on the right, with liveried driver, was not a cab for hire, but probably the private conveyance of a visitor with no small financial means – carriage trade indeed!

Deansgate traffic, around 1932. This photograph from the 1930s confirms the increasing interwar presence of motor transport on Manchester's streets. It was later claimed Deansgate appeared to be 'entirely given over to motor-car salesmen'.

Coach used during the 1913 royal visit to Manchester. The visit by George V to Manchester in 1913 marked the end of a multi-town tour of Lancashire. The photograph was taken by John Cleworth, a Manchester pharmacist. It was reported in a pharmacy trade journal that before photography was a common feature of newspapers, he placed photographs of events that had taken place earlier the same day in his window.

Saloon car for hire, advertising photograph, 1930s. This photographic card is advertising not only the hiring of a car and uniformed driver, but is also promoting the photographer. Harland was listed in trade directories as an undertaker and coffin maker. This firm's address, Gunson Street, was near the busy Oldham Road, where the photographer George Allen had his studio and photographic supply shop.

Manchester Liners vessel *Manchester Port*. In 1898, a fleet of ships was founded to sail from Salford Docks. Their names included 'Manchester', and could be used again for later ships. The photograph shows the *Manchester Port*, the third vessel with this name. It had been built in 1935 and sailed until 1964. It was broken up by the following year.

Manchester Liners vessel *Manchester Port*'s social room. As well as cargo, the ships could carry passengers. A few card games were probably played in this room on the voyages between Canada and Manchester.

Manchester Airport. The airport had opened in 1938 and was known as Ringway, named after a nearby village. It was a municipal airport, owned by Manchester Corporation. Ringway was used by the RAF during the war, but later reverted to civilian aviation. In the 1940s, hope was expressed that it would become the Heathrow of the north. The next decade, a Manchester information bureau publication described it as 'potentially the most important in the country outside London'. By the 1960s, it was a major international airport.

Mancunian Way, 1960s. The photograph shows the Mancunian Way when it was still a motoring novelty. This elevated inner-city motorway had been constructed during the 1960s and was ceremonially opened by Harold Wilson in 1967. The first section linked Chorlton-on-Medlock with Hulme.

Section 5

Learning and the Arts

Victoria University: Manchester

Whitworth Hall, Manchester University. The following photographs record some of Manchester's educational, library and art institutions. Chetham's library has its origins in the seventeenth century, Manchester Grammar School is even older, and the university was a product of the nineteenth century, when there was a recognised need to keep up with advanced education in countries such as Germany and the USA.

Chetham's Hospital buildings. The 'hospital' was a school, established under the will of Humphrey Chetham, a merchant who died in 1653. The buildings were on the site of the old manor house. After the church became collegiate from 1422, they became a residence for priests. The Civil War left them in a ruined state. Chetham's trustees completed the purchase after his death and opened the school for poor boys. Their parents had to be honest and industrious, not 'wandering or idle beggars or rogues'. A library was also endowed.

Humphrey Chetham sculpture (1853) by William Theed, Manchester Cathedral. Chetham was born in Crumpsall and educated at the grammar school. He became a wealthy merchant, working with his brother who was based in London. In 1635, he was made High Sheriff of Lancashire. His name is now commemorated through the library and specialist music school, which was founded in 1969 in the ancient Chetham Hospital buildings.

Chetham's Hospital and Grammar School buildings, early twentieth century. The photograph contrasts the taller Manchester Grammar School elevations with the low-rise buildings of Chetham's Hospital. They both had entrances on Long Millgate. Some bluecoat scholars of Chetham's are also frozen by the camera.

Manchester Grammar School, Long Millgate, from Todd Street. Although the school had been founded in 1515 by Hugh Oldham, Bishop of Exeter, by the twentieth century the buildings were Victorian. Here we see what was known as the 'new building', dating from 1880 and designed by Mills & Murgatroyd. It was linked by the first-floor bridge seen in the distance to the so-called 'old building' of 1870, out of shot. The building seen here was damaged in the war and demolished in the 1950s, although the school had relocated to Rusholme in 1931.

Physics laboratory, Manchester Grammar School, Long Millgate. The 'old building' of 1870 had a drawing hall that could accommodate the whole school and was used for morning assembly. The building also housed the physics laboratory, which was connected via the spiral staircase seen in the photograph to a lecture room above.

Dining room, Manchester Grammar School, Long Millgate. The photograph is from a postcard mailed in 1916. It shows the school's dining hall, located in the basement of the 1870 building. For those who chose not to eat here, the high master wrote in a 1907 city handbook that 'all who prefer it are allowed to get a meal outside in the town'.

Quadrangle buildings, Manchester University, around 1900. The university had begun as Owens College, named after John Owens, a merchant who left money for a non-denominational college of advanced study. It was opened in 1851, housed in Richard Cobden's former home on Quay Street. In 1870, the foundation stone was laid for these new buildings off Oxford Road. The architect was Alfred Waterhouse. Three years later it was ready for students.

Manchester Museum and Whitworth Hall, Oxford Road, early 1900s. In 1880, Owens College became the first member of the federal Victoria University (colleges in Liverpool and Leeds joined later). From 1903, Manchester was an independent university. The nearest building is the Manchester Museum, before the subsequent extension across Coupland Street, seen in the photograph at its junction with Oxford Road. The Whitworth Hall of 1902 is beyond the tower.

Professor Ernest Rutherford and the physics group, Manchester University. Rutherford sits in the centre of the photograph, taken by Oxford Road photographer Edward Ward, whose father had sold microscopy slides and instruments from the same premises. Manchester was then a world centre of excellence in atomic physics. Rutherford had suggested the nuclear model of the atom. On the left end of Rutherford's row sits Hans Geiger from Germany, who designed a particle detector named after him. Henry Moseley, who was killed at Gallipoli in the First World War, is second from the left on the front row. He made a fundamental breakthrough that helped explain atomic structure. At the right end of the first row is James Chadwick, who later discovered the neutron.

Professor Horace Lamb, colleagues and students, Manchester University. This is another photograph by Edward Ward. Lamb is sitting in the middle of the second row from the front. He was an applied mathematician who made important advances in theoretical hydrodynamics and was the author of standard textbooks.

THE UNIVERSITY, MANCHESTER

Whitworth Hall, Manchester University, 1950s postcard. The photograph shows an Oxford Road view of the 1902 Whitworth Hall, named after the Stockport-born engineer and benefactor Joseph Whitworth. On the left is part of the former Students' Union building, which was demolished when a new union building was opened in 1957.

Radio telescope, Manchester University, Jodrell Bank, Cheshire. The photograph is from a postcard mailed in 1963 and so shows the telescope not long after it became operational in 1957. The Manchester University radio astronomer Bernard Lovell was a pioneer in the detection of radio wavelength signals from space, and this steerable radio telescope was later named after him.

Students' Union, Manchester University, 1960s. The building in the photograph dates from 1957, replacing one on a different site – an Edwardian building that was then demolished. The new building, designed by local architect J. S. Beaumont, was described by Nikolaus Pevsner as 'stone-faced and stodgy'. Further into the photograph the refectory is seen, which replaced the old union building, then the Whitworth Hall.

Mary Worthington Wing, Ashburne Hall, Manchester University. The first hall of residence for female students was opened in 1900 at Ashburne House, Victoria Park. Removal was then made to the present Fallowfield site when Edward Behrens bequeathed his home, The Oaks, to the university. The Mary Worthington Wing was built nearby and opened in 1910. It was named after a mill owner's daughter and supporter of women's education. The photograph by Edward Ward shows the building in its early years.

College of Technology, Sackville Street. The photograph is from the 1950s, a decade when the college severed its links with Manchester Corporation, becoming an independent institution called the Manchester College of Science and Technology. In 1966, it took the name University of Manchester Institute of Science and Technology (UMIST), and in 2004 formally merged with Manchester University. It had originated from the Mechanics' Institute of 1824 and by the twentieth century was offering degree-standard technology courses in connection with the university. The building seen here was opened in 1902, then known as the Municipal School of Technology.

Municipal School of Art, Cavendish Street, early 1900s. This art school had started in 1838 as the Manchester School of Design. The building in the photograph was erected 1880–81, around ten years before the school was transferred to Manchester Corporation. Later, it became part of Manchester Metropolitan University.

City Art Gallery, Mosley Street. This building, on the corner of Princess Street, had been designed by Charles Barry, who later worked on the Houses of Parliament. It was erected for the Royal Manchester Institution, founded in 1823, which promoted science, literature and the arts. It was later conveyed to the Corporation for use as an art gallery. Manchester agreed to spend £2,000 a year for twenty years on art works.

The photograph shows an interior view of the City Art Gallery from the early twentieth century. An artist is making a copy of one of the gallery's canvases.

Reference library, former Town Hall, King Street. The building had been erected by a body known as the Police (or Improvement) Commissioners. They acted in a local government role before Manchester became an incorporated borough in 1838. At the time of the photograph the building served as the city's main reference library. It was demolished in 1912, although the columns were moved to Heaton Park.

Reference library interior, former Town Hall, King Street. This view of the library was taken by Robert Banks, one of Manchester's most active photographers during the Edwardian and late Victorian period. When the building was demolished, the reference library moved to huts at Piccadilly.

Central Library, St Peter's Square, 1930s. The new Central Library was designed, along with the Town Hall Extension, by Emanuel Vincent Harris. It was officially opened in 1934 by George V, who was presented with a silver and gold model of the library, fashioned at the School of Art. On the same day, the monarch laid the foundation stone of the Town Hall Extension.

Exhibition hall, Central Library, 1935. The photograph shows an exhibition of the rubber industry and its products. This was probably part educational and part promotional.

John Rylands Library, Deansgate, 1920s. The library had been built for Henriqueta Rylands as a memorial to her late husband, the textile magnate John Rylands. He had been a collector of religious books and his widow wished for a building to house them. She also bought two important private collections of books and manuscripts. The architect was Basil Champneys and work commenced in 1890, taking nine years to complete. It has been part of Manchester University since 1972.

Whitworth Gallery, Whitworth Park, around 1908. The photograph dates from when the building work, which started in 1894, had been recently completed. The gallery, or institute as it was known, had been established by Robert Darbishire, a legatee of the engineer Joseph Whitworth. Its collections were more inclusive than paintings, drawings and sculptures, also including textiles and tapestries. Manchester University acquired the gallery in 1958.

High School for Girls, Dover Street, around 1900. The school opened in 1874, in two houses on Oxford Road. The Dover Street building, designed by Mills & Murgatroyd, dates from 1880–81 and was extended in 1886. The three Pankhurst daughters, Adela, Christabel and Sylvia, attended in the 1890s. After the school had removed to Grangethorpe Road by Platt Fields Park, Manchester University acquired the old building in 1945.

A council school, Levenshulme. The school opened on Errwood Road in 1907, around the date of the photograph. At this time, Levenshulme was administered by an Urban District Council and not yet under Manchester's authority. It was absorbed into the city by 1909 and the school came under the control of the Manchester Education Committee.

Ducie Avenue School, Chorlton-on-Medlock. The school had been opened in 1881 for the Manchester School Board, a directly elected body. It came under the control of the Manchester Education Committee following the Education Act of 1902. The photograph was taken by the Salford-based William Edward Stansfeld Parker, who had taken a photography course after service during the First World War. He specialised in school photographs such as this.

Ravensbury Street School, Clayton, 1937. That year's school photograph was linked to the coronation of George VI, which took place following the abdication of his brother, Edward.

St Bede's College, Alexandra Road South, Whalley Range. The photograph is from a postcard mailed in 1932, although the image is probably a little earlier. St Bede's had been founded in 1876 by the Roman Catholic Bishop of Salford, Herbert Vaughan. At first it was near Oxford Road but soon moved to a site facing Alexandra Park, where it occupied a former aquarium building. The Vaughan Building, seen here, was erected 1877–80 and designed by Dunn & Hansom, an architectural practice that specialised in work on Catholic buildings.

Ardwick Green Industrial School, from a postcard mailed in 1908. At one time this institution was known as the Manchester Ragged and Certified Industrial School. These schools, part of the criminal justice system, were intended to teach youngsters a trade such as joinery, as seen here. The idea was to divert them from a life of crime. The Ardwick industrial school closed in 1922, although the building was later used by St Gregory's, a Catholic high school.

Section 6

Recreation

Palace Theatre, Oxford Street. Away from work, Mancunians had a range of recreational opportunities. Sports such as football could be both watched and played. There were theatre shows and music concerts. Parks had been provided since 1846. Then there was the public house, a home from home in the city centre and suburban district.

LADY-BARN WESLEYAN A. F. C.

T. Crowther   Mr. Baguley   R. Nixon (Tres)   J. Taylor   J. Wildsmith   F. Morris   G. Parker   F. Gratidge   A. Taylor   J. Baguley
W. Baguley   H. Lyth   T. Colton   G. Gratidge (Cap.)   H. Burrows   W. Parker   A. North

Ladybarn Wesleyan football team, 1904–05. In the Edwardian age, football was an established spectator sport, with large crowds attending the professional matches. However, amateur and recreational football was also played. This postcard is of a team from a chapel south of the city centre. It was produced by Robert Scott from Chorlton-on-Medlock, a specialist publisher of sporting subjects.

Military football match, Hyde Road, 1916. This team comprised players from prominent Lancashire clubs, although not all were Lancashire born. Second from the left on the front row is Tommy Boyle, an England international who captained Burnley when they won the FA Cup in 1914. The game was a charity event played at Manchester City's former ground, Hyde Road, against a Yorkshire team. Proceeds went to the Manchester Regiment. The result was 3-0 to the Red Rose. The photographer was a Manchester pharmacist, John Cleworth.

Manchester City, 1954–55. The photograph was taken as product endorsement for the tracksuits the team are wearing. City were losing FA Cup finalists in 1955, but the following season they won the Cup. In the back row, third from the left, is Bert Trautmann, the German goalkeeper. At the right end of the same row stands Don Revie, the future manager of Leeds United and England. Astride the ball sits Roy Paul, the City captain and a Welsh international.

Manchester United, 1962–63. This season saw manager Matt Busby win his first major trophy since the Munich air crash, when they defeated Leicester City in the FA Cup final. Second from right on the front row is Denis Law, who had been a big money signing in the 1962 close season. At the end of that row sits Munich survivor Bobby Charlton. Although United won the Cup, they struggled in the First Division and had to battle against relegation.

FA Cup final replay, Old Trafford, 1911. Manchester United's ground at Old Trafford had opened in February 1910 with a defeat to Liverpool. It was one of the finest football venues in the country. Symbolically, a roof at their old ground in Clayton blew down in a gale shortly before the inaugural match at Old Trafford. In 1911, the stadium was chosen for the FA Cup final replay, where Bradford City beat Newcastle United 1-0. The camera captures the moment when the Bradford captain, Jimmy Speirs, scored the only goal of the game.

Fallowfield Stadium, 1920s. Different sports events have been hosted at Fallowfield. Opened for athletics in 1892, it has also seen cycling, football and rugby. In 1893, the FA Cup final was played here, and there have been Northern Union (later known as Rugby League) Challenge Cup finals. It was acquired by Manchester University and subsequently demolished for halls of residence.

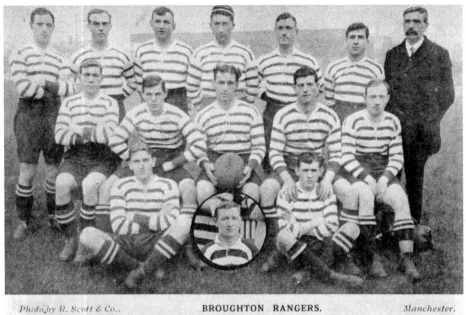

Photo by R. Scott & Co.,   **BROUGHTON RANGERS.**   *Manchester.*

W Harris   A Hirst   Winskill   Gorry   Eddis   Davidson   Taylor *(Tr.)*
    Barlow   'Bouch   J L Clampitt   R Clampitt   Lear
    Mead   E Jones   Warren

Broughton Rangers rugby team. The game known as Rugby League dates from 1895, when a number of northern teams broke away from the Rugby Football Union. The issue was so-called 'broken time payments', the compensating of players for taking time off work to play. The new organisation was called the Northern Rugby Football Union at first. Broughton were one of the original breakaway clubs. In 1933, they left Salford to play at Belle Vue, later changing their name to Belle Vue Rangers. The club finished in 1955. The photograph, by Robert Scott, is not dated but includes some players from the 1911 Challenge Cup-winning team.

Old Trafford cricket ground was home to the Manchester Cricket Club from 1857 and the Lancashire County side from 1864. The pavilion dates from 1895.

Gorton Baths, Hyde Road, around 1910. Public baths were not just for recreational purposes, but could also provide washing facilities when not all homes had their own bathrooms. The baths at Gorton had opened in 1890. The photograph shows first- and second-class entrances. The building was demolished in 2005.

Victoria Baths, Chorlton-on-Medlock. The image is from a photographic postcard mailed in 1909, so the view was taken around the time the baths were opened in 1906 by the Lord Mayor of Manchester. As well as swimming pools, the facilities included private baths and a laundry. After closure in 1993, the building was not maintained and fell into a state of disrepair. However, supporters, assisted by lottery money and other funds, have worked to give new life to the building.

Levenshulme Public Baths and Washhouse photographed when they were new – they opened in 1921. The photograph is from an original print used by an Ardwick postcard publisher, James L. Brown, who was active in the 1920s.

Tennis group, around 1910. The identity of these tennis players is not given on the photograph. However, the photographer is named in a 1911 trade directory as Charles Bernard Owen who had a studio on Barlow Moor Road, Didsbury.

Palace Theatre, Oxford Street. When the *Manchester Evening News* reported on the opening night in May 1891, it asserted that the city had 'approved of the latest effort that had been made to amuse it'. The building was designed by the Salford-born architect, Alfred Darbyshire, who was also an artist, writer and amateur actor.

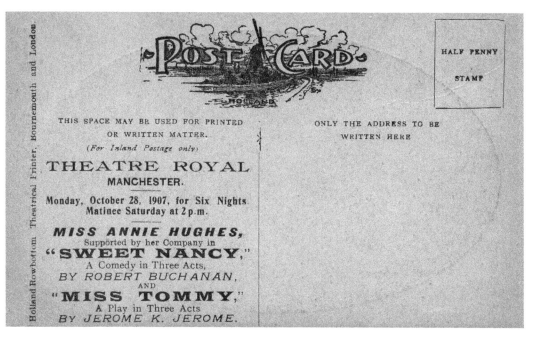

Theatre Royal advertising postcard, 1907. This theatre had been opened on Peter Street in 1845. It replaced an earlier Theatre Royal in Fountain Street, which was destroyed by fire the previous year. The front of the card has a portrait of the actress Annie Hughes who starred in this stage production in Edwardian Manchester.

Hippodrome, Oxford Street. The Hippodrome was built for Oswald Stoll, a major UK theatre owner. It had opened in 1904 as a variety theatre, with stabling for animals and the possibility of putting on aquatic shows. The building to its right, occupied by Patteson's, a supplier of headstones and various other items of stoneware, gives an idea of earlier Oxford Street architecture. It was demolished for the Picture House cinema of 1911. The Hippodrome closed in 1935.

Hippodrome, Ardwick. This theatre was built for Oswald Stoll, who also opened the Hippodrome on Oxford Street in the same year, 1904. The Ardwick venue was at first called the Empire, but when the Oxford Street theatre closed in 1935, the name was transferred to this building, as seen in the photograph. It closed in 1961 and was subsequently demolished.

Gaumont cinema, Oxford Street, 1930s. The Hippodrome theatre closed in 1935 and was demolished. On the site, the cinema in the photograph was built and opened that same year. It closed in 1974, was later used as a nightclub, and was then itself demolished. The photograph was taken by Arthur Harold Clarke, who has recorded the building when still pristine.

Piccadilly cinema, 1920s. This view of Piccadilly has, on the left of the frame, the recently built Piccadilly cinema and restaurant. It opened in 1922 on the site of the demolished Mosley Hotel and closed in 1937. The building was converted to retail use and for years housed a Littlewoods store.

Alhambra theatre and cinema, Ashton Old Road, Higher Openshaw. The Alhambra had opened in 1909 as a variety theatre, but within a few years part of the theatre was converted to a cinema called the Alhambra Pavilion. After non-cinematic uses, the building was demolished in 2009. The junction on the left is with Old Lane. The shops include an optician, tobacconist, grocer and the baker Fentem's.

Gramophone concert, Queen's Park, around 1908. Not all entertainment took place in large purpose-built theatres and concert halls. The photograph shows a scene in a Manchester park where a gramophone concert is being given from the bandstand. The announcement on the left reads 'CARUSO IS SINGING'.

Beswick Prize Band, possibly 1920s. This band had been formed in 1894 and entered a number of brass band contests, including at Belle Vue. In 1965, they merged with the Moston band. They also provided match entertainment at both City and United. The image was by Foulds & Gleaves, photographers from Ashton New Road.

Hans Richter, conductor, Hallé Orchestra. Richter, a friend of Richard Wagner, was the Hallé's conductor from 1899 to 1911. He had been born in the Austro-Hungarian Empire and studied in Vienna. He retired in 1911 because of poor eyesight and died in 1916 at Bayreuth.

Botanical gardens, Old Trafford. The Manchester Botanical and Horticultural Society had been founded in 1827. The idea was to provide gardens and greenhouses, not only for recreational purposes, but also to further scientific research. Land from the de Trafford family was conveyed in 1829, then leased to the society. The site chosen at Old Trafford was on the advice of John Dalton, the scientist, who had judged it on the basis that prevailing winds would keep industrial smoke pollution away.

Palm house, botanical gardens, Old Trafford. Plant houses and conservatories were erected and specimens from around the world were brought to the gardens. However, by the early twentieth century, subscription income had fallen. Unsuccessful attempts were made to interest Stretford District Council and Manchester City Council in buying the site. It was then leased for the White City amusement park.

White City entrance, Chester Road, Old Trafford, 1907. Heathcote & Brown, proprietors of the White City amusement park, had acquired the land from the Royal Botanical Society. The park opened in 1907, created in the short time of just ten weeks. Amusements included a figure-of-eight roller coaster, water chute and helter-skelter. The entrance seen in the photograph was originally the gateway to the botanical gardens.

White City, Old Trafford. This composition, taken at the White City, is not too revealing in its caption, 'A Study'. The photographer is given as 'C. D'. This was probably Charles Downs of Cooke Street (later named Stanley Road), Old Trafford, who is noted on other White City photographs.

Alexandra Park entrance, Alexandra Road South. Manchester's first two public parks were opened in 1846. These were Queen's Park in Harpurhey and Philips Park, Bradford. They had been financed by private subscription and then conveyed to Manchester Corporation. Alexandra Park at Whalley Range was created between 1868 and 1870.

Heaton Park, former Town Hall colonnade. When Manchester Corporation purchased Heaton Hall and grounds in 1902, it more than doubled the then total acreage of its parks and open spaces. Its large area made it suitable, according to an Edwardian chairman of the Parks Committee, for 'galas, fêtes, military parades and drills, mass meetings etc'. The columns of the old Town Hall in King Street were erected in the park following demolition in 1912.

Whitworth Park and some of its visitors, from a postcard mailed in 1910. The park was named after the engineer Joseph Whitworth. It had been opened in 1890 and leased to Manchester Corporation in 1904. Since 1958, it has been owned by Manchester University.

Platt Fields Park boating lake, from a postcard mailed in 1912. Platt Hall and its grounds were purchased by Manchester Corporation in 1908, and the land made into a public park with the help of the unemployed. A lake of 6.5 acres was excavated, with the spoil used to create an island in the centre. The park was formally opened in 1910 by the Lord Mayor of Manchester, Charles Behrens.

Parsonage Gardens in the interwar period. This compact haven between Deansgate and the River Irwell was once the site of a church, St Mary's, which was consecrated in 1756. It had been demolished during the nineteenth century, leaving this spot of tranquillity. St Mary's Hospital was at one time located nearby on South Parade, and took its name from the church. Neighbouring street names include St Mary's Parsonage and St Mary's Street.

Bowling green, Chorlton Park, Chorlton-cum-Hardy, possibly in the 1950s. Manchester's parks included sporting facilities such as tennis courts and bowling greens. The clubhouse, seen on the left, was once a farm building connected with Hough End Hall.

Fox Tavern, Clayton Lane, Openshaw. The public house was a vital ingredient of community life. The photograph shows a group of regulars posed before a pub outing. The destination, unfortunately, is not given on the print. The Ardwick-based Chesters Brewery name is partially revealed on the window. The pub, which was at the junction with Ridings Street, closed in 2003 and was demolished.

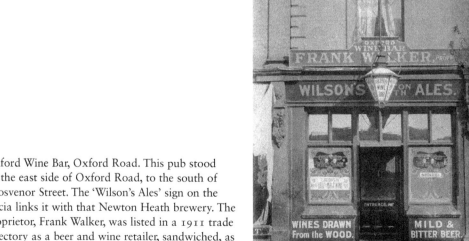

Oxford Wine Bar, Oxford Road. This pub stood on the east side of Oxford Road, to the south of Grosvenor Street. The 'Wilson's Ales' sign on the fascia links it with that Newton Heath brewery. The proprietor, Frank Walker, was listed in a 1911 trade directory as a beer and wine retailer, sandwiched, as it were, between a milliner and ladies' outfitter.

The Blue Bell Inn, Barlow Road, Levenshulme, around 1910. This building stood on the south side of Barlow Road, by Cromwell Grove. The licensee at this time was called John Blomiley. In the 1930s, a new Blue Bell Inn was built.

Metropolitan-Vickers social club, Moss Road, Stretford. The photograph is by Arthur Harold Clarke, and probably dates from the 1930s. Large companies might offer their workers amenities such as this, which included an entertainment hall, bar, billiards and an outside area for bowls and tennis.

Whit Walks, Albert Square. The Whitsuntide walks in Manchester go back to the beginning of the nineteenth century, when Sunday school children assembled in St Ann's Square and walked to the Collegiate Church (later cathedral). By Edwardian times, when this photograph was taken by Robert Banks, they gathered in Albert Square.

Whit Walks, Albert Square. The tradition of Whit Week was that Anglicans walked on Whit Monday and Roman Catholics on the Friday. The photograph is another by Robert Banks. A rubber stamp on the reverse indicates that they were also sold through Bednal Bros, a Market Street bookseller and stationer.

Whit Walks, Piccadilly. Crowds came into the city centre and lined the streets to watch the walks. For photographers such as Robert Banks, the business case was compelling. Just one image would include numerous people, whose families were potential purchasers. This photograph has a number – '40' – which is how a particular shot was identified for purchase. It also suggests the number of images that were made.

Whit Walks, possibly east Manchester. Whit Walks also took place in the districts. The exact location of this procession is not given, although the photographer John Fieldsend had a business address on Gorton Lane, Gorton. Pre-First World War trade directories list him as a chemist.

Victoria Street during the visit to Manchester by the Prince of Wales in 1921. Royal visits brought large numbers onto the streets to view and wave. This scene is from a visit by the Prince of Wales in July 1921. The nearest car, carrying the lord mayor, is turning into Fennel Street from Victoria Street. The motorcade at this point was on its way to Chetham's Hospital and Manchester Grammar School, then on Long Millgate.

A T. Seymour Meade-decorated wagon. Recreation took different guises. This photograph doesn't reveal the location or the event. It seems likely though that the subject is ready to join a parade or other festivity. T. Seymour Meade had a number of grocery stores in Manchester.

Section 7

Suburbs

High Street (later Hathersage Road), Chorlton-on-Medlock. When Manchester was incorporated as a borough in 1838, it included Ardwick, Beswick, Cheetham, Chorlton-on-Medlock, Hulme and Manchester itself. It later took in other neighbouring townships, which increased the municipal area and also altered the shape of the city. The following photographs are a selection of images from the districts beyond the city centre.

St Mary's Hospital, Oxford Road. Chorlton-on-Medlock became home to Manchester University and also to major hospitals. This photographic postcard was mailed in 1911, so both the St Mary's Hospital building of 1909 was recent as was that of the Royal Infirmary (formally opened in 1909), seen in the distance. St Mary's, a hospital for women and children, has a history going back to 1790. It had several changes of location, one of which was near to St Mary's Church, off Deansgate, and gave the hospital its name.

Manchester Royal Infirmary, Oxford Road, around 1911. The infirmary had stood at Piccadilly since the eighteenth century. However, a decision was taken to build a new hospital on Oxford Road, on land offered by the university. This meant that university medical students could gain clinical experience just across the road. The building, described as in a 'Greenwich baroque' style, was ready by 1908 and ceremonially opened the following year.

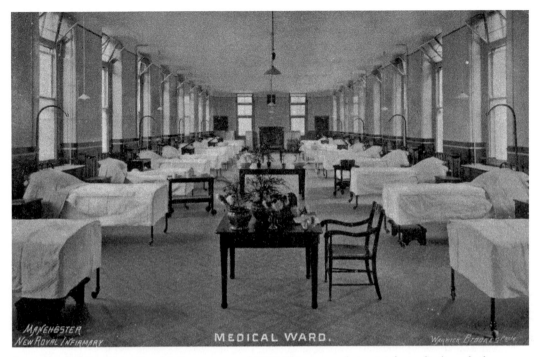

A ward in the Manchester Royal Infirmary, around 1908. This postcard view is of a medical ward when still in a patient-free state. The image was based on an original photograph by Warwick Brookes, who had a studio across the road from the infirmary at the junction of Oxford Road and Denmark Road.

Oxford Road photographer Warwick Brookes. The photographer, who recorded the Royal Infirmary when it was newly built, is using the reverse of a studio portrait to advertise his work. He is also disclaiming any association with another photographer of the same name – his cousin!

116

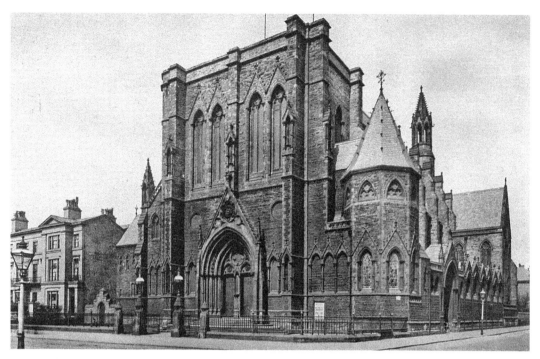

Holy Name Church, Oxford Road. The foundation stone of this church had been laid in 1869 by William Turner, the first Roman Catholic bishop of Salford. It was designed by Joseph Hansom and his son. Hansom Snr had given his name to the two-wheeled cab. The church was ready by 1871, staffed by Jesuit priests. The photograph shows the building before the tower was heightened in 1928.

Holy Name Church, Oxford Road, with a new tower around 1928. The original plan was for a steeple but this was not built. However, Adrian Gilbert Scott designed an addition to the existing tower. This was completed in 1928 and dedicated as a memorial to a former rector, Bernard Vaughan.

Nelson Street, Chorlton-on-Medlock. This street, off Oxford Road, is seen here most likely around the 1920s. The view is looking in an easterly direction, with Oxford Road behind the photographer. The street has a look that would have been familiar to the Pankhurst family, who lived here from 1898 until 1907. Their home was at No. 62, out of shot in the distance on the left. In 1903, the Women's Social and Political Union was founded there.

David Lloyd George. One of Manchester's most famous sons was the Liberal politician David Lloyd George, born in 1863 to Welsh parents, who lived at Chorlton-on-Medlock. His family moved to Wales shortly after. Lloyd George achieved ministerial high office, becoming prime minister during the First World War. In 1918, he was made a freeman of the city of Manchester.

Plymouth Grove, 1920s. By the middle years of the nineteenth century, Plymouth Grove had become a select address, with villas for the professional classes. The novelist Elizabeth Gaskell lived here from 1850. By Edwardian times, though, things had changed. Louis Hayes wrote in his 1905 reminiscences that grand old residences had been joined by 'rows of ordinary-looking, cheap-rented houses' – perhaps he meant ones such as those on the right. The tower of the former Wesleyan church is on the left, by Hyde Grove.

Stockport Road, Ardwick. At the beginning of the nineteenth century Ardwick was a semi-rural retreat. However, by the end of that century it had been transformed into a district of trains, trams and workers' housing. The photograph is by Devonshire Street, on the left, with the Octagon Congregational Church opposite.

Stockport Road, Longsight. When the photograph was taken, Longsight was considered a suburb for the white-collar classes. Even after the Second World War, it was described as 'a middle-class residential area'. The view is from just north of the junction with Plymouth Grove, looking in the direction of Ardwick.

Dickenson Road, Longsight. This Edwardian photograph, taken at the junction with Birch Lane on the left, gives an idea of a leafy residential Longsight road. In the distance is the busy Stockport road and its shops.

Ashton Old Road, Openshaw. This main road carried traffic to and from the east of Manchester. The photograph is from a postcard mailed in 1922. The building on the left was the Gransmoor pub. Gransmoor Road is the next junction, where the signs for Bovril, Oxo and Cadbury's are seen. The view is towards Fairfield with the road then continuing to Ashton-under-Lyne.

Arthur Balfour, MP for Manchester East. The aristocratic, intellectual and aloof-mannered Balfour represented the parliamentary constituency of Manchester East from 1885 until 1906. That latter year, his Conservative party was defeated by the Liberals in a general election. During part of his time as a Manchester MP, he was also prime minister from 1902 to 1905.

Alexandra Road, Moss Side. The camera is aiming south from the junction with Moss Lane West, on the right. Further on, the road becomes Alexandra Road South and passes Alexandra Park. The shop on the left is a branch of T. Seymour Mead, a grocer and tea merchant, with stores in other parts of Manchester. On the right, by Moss Lane West, is J. R. Blair & Sons, wine and spirits merchants.

Willow Bank Military Hospital, Moss Lane East, Moss Side. This photograph of patients and staff was taken in May 1918, not long before the Armistice. The photographer was a Manchester pharmacist named John Cleworth. A 1931 pharmacy trade journal stated that during the First World War he was the 'official military photographer for the Manchester area'.

Moseley Road Military Hospital, Fallowfield. This First World War hospital was housed in a requisitioned school building. The photograph is from a postcard sent in August 1916. The message reads, 'This is where my brother is. It is so sad to see them but he is getting on alright.'

Wilmslow Road, Rusholme, around 1910. The township of Rusholme became part of Manchester in 1885. The photograph was taken near the Old Hall Lane tram stop, on the left. The sign says that trams stop by request. The relocation of Manchester Grammar School to Rusholme was still twenty years in the future. Platt Fields was opened around this time as a public park.

Victoria Park, Longsight entrance. This twentieth-century photograph shows toll gates at an entrance to this private and exclusive development of secluded villas. The estate was ceremonially opened in 1837, represented from 1845 by a Victoria Park Trust. The main road in front of the gates is Plymouth Grove. Opposite, beyond the barriers, is Daisy Bank Road. The tolls went in 1954, but in the 1940s it was still described as 'Manchester's curio – a toll-protected private estate built astride one of the main arterial roads.'

St Chrysostom's Church, Victoria Park. This Anglican church had been consecrated in 1877. However, in 1904 a fire caused major structural damage. Electrical wiring had been suspected as a cause. It was rebuilt by 1906. The photograph from Anson Road shows the aftermath of the fire.

124

Didsbury in the early twentieth century. The view is looking south along Wilmslow Road. The former Didsbury station is off frame to the left, where the Dr Rhodes memorial clock tower of 1911 has yet to be unveiled. We see two waiting hansom cabs and a cabmen's shelter. The transport in the main road is also equine rather than motorised. Didsbury was absorbed into Manchester in 1904.

St Christopher's Church, Withington. This Anglican parish had been created in 1932 for the Old Moat estate, an interwar housing development. St Christopher's, at the end of Moorgate Avenue, off Princess Road, was opened in 1935. The photograph by Arthur Harold Clarke, shows the building when new. Structural problems caused it to be demolished in 1995.

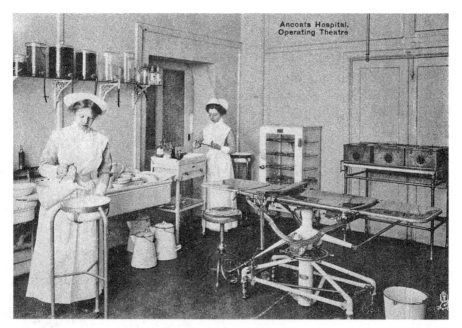

Ancoats Hospital in the early twentieth century. Medical provision in this working-class and industrial district had been provided by the Ardwick and Ancoats Dispensary of 1828. However, this was for outpatients and home visits. By the 1870s, and with a new building, there were inpatient beds. The name was changed to the descriptive, but wordy, Ancoats Hospital and Ardwick and Ancoats Dispensary.

St Casimir's Church, Oldham Road, Collyhurst. The photograph was taken when Cardinal August Hlond, the head of the Catholic Church in Poland, visited Manchester in October 1930. St Casimir's was housed in a former Methodist chapel, a building since demolished. It was used by Poles, Lithuanians and Ukrainians. The Roman Catholic Bishop of Salford, Thomas Henshaw, is standing fourth from the right. The photographer, local man George Allen, had a studio on Oldham Road.

Crumpsall Lane, Crumpsall. This district to the north of the city centre was the birthplace of Humphrey Chetham, whose name is memorialised in the music school and library. One of the local employers was the Co-operative Wholesale Society, which established a biscuit factory here. Crumpsall became part of Manchester in 1890. This photograph of Crumpsall Lane, which has a junction with the busy Middleton Road, captures a leafy Edwardian scene.

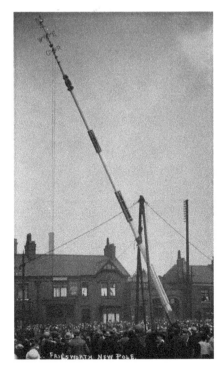

Failsworth Pole, 1924. The Newton Heath photographer Berne Lancelot Pearson made the short journey into neighbouring Failsworth to get this image. One of the local landmarks was the Failsworth Pole, historically a political show of Church and King loyalty. The photograph shows the last wooden pole being raised in August 1924. This blew down in 1950, to be replaced in 1958 by a pole above a brick-built clock tower.

Acknowledgements

Books such as this owe their primary existence to the photographers of a bygone age, who have bequeathed their work to later generations. A generalised acknowledgement is offered here. The images have been copied from materials in the compiler's own collection of old photographs, vintage postcards and antiquarian books. These have mostly been acquired from specialist dealers, whether at fairs or through internet purchases. Those who have assisted in the search for Manchester items include Chris Breen, Grenville Collins, Julia Couchman, Stephen Dignum, Xavier Goossens, Chris Newall and Lena Ottosson. Apologies to anyone who may have been omitted. Finally, I wish to thank Amberley Publishing for their interest shown in this Manchester project.